and now

pap<

Jagriti Choudhry

BookLeaf
Publishing

and now it's on paper © 2022 Jagriti
Choudhry

All rights reserved.

Jagriti Choudhry asserts the moral right to
be identified as author of this work.

Presentation by *BookLeaf Publishing*

Web: www.bookleafpub.com

E-mail: info@bookleafpub.com

ISBN: 9789395756723

First edition 2022

DEDICATION

To myself.

ACKNOWLEDGEMENT

These poems have been possible with all my life experiences. The people I have come across in all these years, and the places I have visited have played a vital role in shaping my thoughts.
I learnt a lot about the english, my second language by my mother, an English teacher by profession.
Special Thanks to dear friend Julia Hastie for volunteering to proof read my work.

PREFACE

The poems are a vehicle for me to introspect and have a deeper connection with myself and the world. I have grown up in an upper-middle-class family in India and lived with my parents before moving to the UK. The self-discovery in a land abroad and independent life provided me a playground to explore the variety of things that varied drastically between two countries, which has been mentioned in the poems.

The other poems delve into the themes of loneliness, unrequited love, anxiety but mainly self-reflection . Some of these are poems are personal while I borrowed inspiration for others from the lives and instances I have heard about. Coming out into the world, living on my own and still seeking myself, these poems have been a monumental tool to help me understand myself better.

Dinner

Can you please stay the night
I promise tonight there won't be a fight.
I am tired of the justifications.
I know you must be too .

I've made the bed
The sheets are fresh.
The incense sticks are still there ,
I'll put them on
Make some tea
And bake some bread.

I've not put your plate to use in weeks,
It's got an adamant stain
Of the sauce we made last,
I couldn't bother to clean it.

There are a few flowers I brought
But dear me
Nothing can compare
Your beauty.

What else?
Hmm I brought some alcohol
You can have some if you'd like
For me it isn't them,

To be intoxicated in,
It's your eyes.

I'll stop with my clichéd rants,
But words are all I have you see.

What if I expect you to come
And get ready , and
You don't come,
Oh that would be
Another tragedy.

Time

And each time I find happiness I'm startled
by the thought of its transiency.
The best moments are ruined by
 the momentary gaze into the future.
The happiness I find are in those who are mortal,
flawed and complicated-humans.

Their hands are tender, soft, the ones I want to
hold,
but for how long?
The words they speak are melodious,endearing
but for how long?
Their eyes are enchanting,
they captivate me and seek me too,
but for how long?

Eventually,
gradually,
ultimately
it's always time that lasts,
whilst I am still here,
they have abandoned me
and are lost.

Silence

A simple yet powerful tool
At the disposal of all
Yet seldom used.

A synonym for peace
An affirmation of distress
A desperate need for those in a raucous world
A friend of those living in solitude.

Are you the one?

Me and my eyes
have longed to see
a blissful, beautiful, beloved
a someone I can call mine unapologetically.

For days and nights
Through countries
And times.
My heart has searched recklessly.

And each time I find a shadow of
a budding lover,
and we share a perhaps future,
I am struck with my haunting past
and its daunting memory.

And then I am convinced
she, like them is ephemeral.
Sooner or later my flaws shall
mark this relationships doom,
left behind shall be misery.

Maybe I need to stop looking
stop hunting
stop chasing,

it is a work of fate.
For they say,
it happens
In the most unexpected ways.

Oh my dear

Only the privileged are meant to be
Whilst you, my dear, are not ready.
Toxic traits have poisoned* you deep within
You can't take this ride steady.

Been in an exhausting cycle of unrequited love,
you have incited,
I wish you tried better, my child.

Your demons within, they come out eventually
There's only so much the poor closet can keep!

Your efforts are always futile,
there has never been a lover for you
you only have half-hearted by your side.

So pack your bag of affection,
and move again into another hemisphere.
There is nobody who'd want it here
my dear.

I am not yours anymore

I'm caught in a web I've made myself
I've grown up in a web too
Whilst other kids walked hand in hand
Here I was on my own carrying "you".

"You" were just a regular person
Until you weren't
Slowly my days began with "you" and ended
with "you"
Some years passed and you went away too

Here I was stuck in a gloom
Seeking now another form of "you"
Along came a new person
And she was so much better too.

With her words and her deeds
She had me under her spell
She became the "one"
Only until 2 years later she broke me, as well.

With prayers and songs
I longed for refuge.
I wanted the world to stop,
For my heart was in pain,

But time has never been a friend
And my wish was in vain.
Each day passed and so did my older self
Now I'm quaint
I have become someone else.

For Her

You profoundly bit my heart
and the scar remains still.
It was you, and then her
and then the one who came after.

There have been so many of you,
each biting off parts of me,
Each of you scraping parts of me,
And I, the relinquished fool, to seek your misery.

Oh my lovely, tender heart,
it thought you were the soul
that can help it heal and
make it feel whole.

Creeping into my memories and my behaviours
everyday,
'she', I could have worked it out with
is now astray.
It is all because of you, your venomous doing
It was you and then her and then
the one who came after

A fugitive of your wrong doing,
my therapist tells me I am well.

I am indeed better, I don't want you back
and live through your hell.
I can spit words to cease my anguish
And the mistrust you embodied.
But I have gone past it now.
It is only the agony chasing me around.
It was you and then her, and then the one who
came after.

The Journey

In a little part of the main city
Where the streets were so narrow and close
I could hear my neighbours
When their guests were at their door.

Calling aloud on the streets
vegetable vendors, salesman of saris,
fresh fruitseller and saffron saints.

The sun in the summers
and scorching heat
the temperature boiling enough
to have roads in the noon
quiet and solitary.

the winter smog
and a hot cup of tea
dipping my biscuit into
and sipping an
aromatic awakening.

I have left behind my all of these
I have left behind what reined me.
And eloped

into a Kingdom of dreams.

II

Here they celebrate Pride
they don't ask me "what are you?"
they dont make grim faces at the undercut
they dont have a problem with my tattoo.

There is now a pride flag in my room
I have chosen my pronouns too
While there is often a gloom,
leaving home wasnt easy
but it was something I ought to do.

How long should I have been caged?
I think everyone deserves a chance to come
through
There is always a choice as they say,
I just had to dig deep
and find the courage to breakthrough.

Sun and the Moon

Constant lovers
them two,
generally I see the sun in the morning
and later the moon.

they stay in the
same sky
together
yet
apart
away from each other
gazing at each other
during the day
but later the sun goes afar.

Seldom do they intertwine
only once in a while.
People call it the 'eclipse'!
oh how wonderful
we dare not see them
as they unite.

That is how the most beautiful
precious

monumental
that ever existed stays,
concealed from the eyes
of the world
hidden away!

Mother

Oh mother
I am sorry to have brought you shame
In a society, you and father have worked hard
To make a name.

My choices are peculiar
they have braced me for failure.
I am inclined to the unnatural love mother,
the one that fits the frame of a taboo.
"How can two women even have kids?"
"Just marry a man, it ain't too much to do!"

My dreams my desires
Have never been orthodox
Oh mother how I wish
I were better than
All the worries I brought.

And I have tried
To make life easier
But it just wouldn't abide
I need a little love, it isn't too much to ask, right?

I know you may feel I am In a dilemma
But I have loved only the fairer sex

It has always been that way maa.

You love me so much, mother
So I think if you'd ask me
I'd make a sacrifice.
You can ask me to give it up,
And I will.
And I shall live in exile.

Moonlight

The moon is too bright tonight
It's peeping through the window
Tell it off please
I don't need the moonlight.

It's been away for days
And now it's got time for me
No use
I'm whole now
I don't need it's sympathy

I have no place in my life
For half hearted lovers,
Seldom near me
And always far from sight,
You've disappointed me
My love,
our love has reached its night.

Endings

There are no tomorrows
for you and me,
our journey was short-lived.
we still have miles to go,
but our roads are running in different directions,
mine is towards the horizons,
whilst you are chasing sunsets.

There is no respite for me in you,
there is no solace for you in me.
I need time away from here now,
let me pack my shattered dreams.

Welcome to UK

I did not know
such a place
existed in reality.
you don't have to be
a boy
or a girl
you can be an other.

There is a mother
with two kids and a wife,
there are two men, in love,
getting married by the sea-side.

Oh how blissful and splendid
seems like there is another world,
if you can step out of the trenches.

funny how borders can part the land,
and the lives of those on either side.
At least before I head back to reality,
I have witnessed a real paradise!

I am exhausted

Under the shower
i stood
a second passed,
and I for once
in a long long time
were blank.
nothing else to be
no worries
or memories
just an empty
second
of existence.

I opened my eyes
and with a long sigh
started my
introspection.
How long have I
been longing
holding desires
working continuously
and forgotten
about existing.

A momentary pause

maybe that is all
we need.
not any lover
not any.

Answers

For all it takes
is to be unlike Oedipus.
stop chasing the answers
and let there be fuss.

Perhaps uncertainty is the answer,
and hope
the only chance for a disdained soul
to thrive in life and advance.

Whilst prancing on your journey
you ought to be astounded,
wandering in the abyss
or gliding in the mountains,
there is no pride in
being all sorted and sounded.

I love me

The first instance I saw you
I knew it
that you were different.
Unlike all those who had been,
oh how I tried to be
someone you'd fancy!

I think it was the way you looked
or maybe the way you walked
but nothing struck me
as hard
as your smile when you and I talked.

I was lovestruck and doomed
I knew it right away
I knew I was on the same path
of devastation
but so is love, it has comes in all nasty ways.

And my intuition was right
I was obsessed with you
thinking of you day and night.
But if it were wrong then how else are you
meant to love?

If I were to think of someone else
and be able to take my mind off you.
If I were to be looking at other prospects
and letting you be just another friend too!
how is It love? I do not understand the
moderation
it sucks!

I am sorry If I overwhelm you
but its just how I am.
I wont change myself
I am splendid and
in love with the idea of love
and I am in love with myself
just how I am.

I cant give you what you want

Life's about choices
And you chose the life
Without me in it.

Your decisions show your love
You don't have to pretend anymore
I've had enough.
You have just uttered the words
My last lover said to me
And I still regret
To even have her exist,
Even in the faintest
Of my memory.

So this is it.
It seems,
You have made a decision
And I'd like to bear the consequences.
Love is not for the faint hearts
It takes a lifetime
To be worthy of a lover
You too had to play a part.

Alas you were mistake.

As I look in hindsight.
I wish
I wish
I was not a fool
Yet again.
I wish
I wasn't captivated by those eyes.
But the damage is now done
It's me who will again have to
Be the one
Mending my heart.

Good bye to you,
I won't wish you anything
For you don't exist for me now,
You've given me sorrows to dwelve in.

And guess what?
despite all of these
lines I've said in your disgrace
My heart would still sleep with your thoughts
tonight.
Oh how frivolous this petty business of love is
When in the world will I ever get it right !!

And I wonder here

And I wonder here
who is there?

In those lonely nights when you are up alone
trying to fight those demons, which you've
realized are not under your bed, never were,
but inside your head.
They've confiscated you and your thoughts,
your mind and you are now lost.
Who's there to help?

In those cold days when your sunshine's away,
when you are looking for warmth
and searching recklessly in the midst of the
storm,
while struggling hard to survive
and stay alive.
Who's there to rescue?

In those seasons when the trees look grotesque,
when you see no flower bloom,
no escape from the gloom.
When the chatter and the noise is louder than
your voice
and your screams are unheard.

Who's there to shelter?

In that phase of your life, in those days and those
nights and those seasons you realize,
You are there.
You are there to your help, to your rescue, to
your shelter, and no one. No one else.
None wanted, and none needed.

Ingram Content Group UK Ltd.
Milton Keynes UK
UKHW021053100423
419916UK00015B/702